George Herbert Rodwell

**My Wife's Out**

George Herbert Rodwell

**My Wife's Out**

ISBN/EAN: 9783337816711

Printed in Europe, USA, Canada, Australia, Japan

Cover: Foto ©Thomas Meinert / pixelio.de

More available books at **www.hansebooks.com**

# MY WIFE'S OUT.

## AN ORIGINAL FARCE, IN ONE ACT.

### BY G. HERBERT RODWELL.

*First performed at the Theatre Royal Covent Garden, October 2, 1843.*

## Dramatis Personæ.

[See page 7.

| | |
|---|---|
| Mr. Scumble | Mr. Keeley |
| Mr. Augustus Dobbs | Mr. A. Wigan. |
| Mrs. Scumble | Miss J. Mordaunt. |
| Betty | Mrs. Keeley. |

TIME OF REPRESENTATION.—Forty Minutes.

**No. 699. Dicks' Standard Plays.**

# MY WIFE'S OUT.

## AN ORIGINAL FARCE, IN ONE ACT.

### BY G. HERBERT RODWELL.

*First performed at the Theatre Royal Covent Garden, October 2, 1843.*

### Dramatis Personæ.

[See page 7.

| | |
|---|---|
| Mr. Scumble | Mr. Keeley |
| Mr. Augustus Dobbs | Mr. A. Wigan. |
| Mrs. Scumble | Miss J. Mordaunt. |
| Betty ... | Mrs. Keeley. |

TIME OF REPRESENTATION.—Forty Minutes.

No. 699. Dicks' Standard Plays.

# COSTUME.

SCUMBLE.—A blouse, blue, edged with white cord—neatly made black trousers—shoes and silk stockings—a Greek cap with gold tassel. 2nd dress: Blue dress coat—handsome waistcoat—trousers, &c., same as first dress—no cap.

DOBBS.—Dark brown loose coat, fastened at the throat, frogs and braid down the front—a German pipe hanging at one side of the breast, a tobacco pouch at the other—light coloured foreign travelling cap—trousers to come well over the foot.

MRS. SCUMBLE.—Neat white bonnet—dove-coloured satin pelisse, shawl. 2nd dress: Foraging cap—handsome Chesterfield coat—blue trousers with red band down the sides—boots and brass spurs. 3rd Dress: Same as first.

BETTY.—A neat servant's dress—clean holland apron. Afterward with bonnet and shawl.

---

## STAGE DIRECTIONS.

EXITS AND ENTRANCES.—R. means Right; L. Left; D. F. Door in Flat; R. D. Righ Door; L. D. Left Door; S. E. Second Entrance; U. E. Upper Entrance; M. D. Middle Door; L. U. E. Left Upper Entrance; R. U. E. Right Upper Entrance; L. S. E. Left Second Entrance; P. S. Prompt Side; O. P. Opposite Prompt.

RELATIVE POSITIONS.—R. means Right; L. Left; C. Centre; RC., Right of Centre; L.C. Left of Centre.

R.          RC.          C          LC.          L.

*₊* The Reader is supposed to be on the Stage, facing the Audience.

# MY WIFE'S OUT.

SCENE.—*A Handsome Room, in part fitted up as an Artist's Study. Pictures hanging and standing about the room—some finished, others in progress—on an easel, R. C., is a large unfinished picture of Actæon and Diana—Actæon with the stag's horns on his head—a high stool before it, on which is lying an artist's palette and resting stick—door, C.—a door, R.—another L. 2 E.—a table, L. C.—a sideboard, L., and three or four chairs.*

*Enter* BETTY *and* MRS. SCUMBLE, L. D.—*Mrs. Scumble is dressed in a dove-coloured pelisse and white bonnet, as if about to go out—she carries in her hand an open letter.*

*Mrs. S.* No, Betty, this I never will forgive—never, never! What, my husband write to a little French bonnet-maker, who works at the second-floor window opposite, inviting her, during my absence too, to come over and sit to him as a model for his Diana, for that odious picture there? It would serve him right if I made him sit for Actæon himself.

*Betty.* Law, ma'am! if I'd a thought that you would have taken on so, I'd a never have given you that letter. I thought it would comfort you to know what was going on.

*Mrs. S.* So it does—it's a perfect comfort to me! and, oh, what a good, kind-hearted soul you must be, Betty, to open my eyes to all my misery! And only to think now, remembering that this was his birthday, I've had this miniature—look, Betty, this miniature of myself, painted on the sly, on purpose for him, the naughty, naughty fellow!

*Betty.* (*Looking at it.*) How very like, to be sure! capital likeness! it's exactly the colour of your black velvet dress, isn't it? But do you know, ma'am, I don't believe Mr. Scumble is really wicked, not downright wicked.

*Mrs. S.* Why do you believe so, Betty?

*Betty.* Because he has never taken the slightest liberty with me, and I know what wicked masters are, I can tell you. I think it's only his vanity. You know we've a very fine, tall, handsome lodger in our second floor, Signor Cornuto, the celebrated French horn player, with as much hair upon his face as would stuff an arm-chair. (*Horn heard without.*) Hark, he's playing now. Well, I can tell you as how that little forward French minx is always ogling the signor; and as she throws her sheep's eyes across the street, I think master has caught one or two on 'em, and thought they were for him, and that made him write to her. Now, if I were you, ma'am, I'd punish him soundly, and then forgive him, for he really is a duck of a little man.

*Mrs. S.* Betty, I'll trouble you to look somow here else for your ducks if you please. But what's to be done—how can I punish him? I should fe quite happy if I could only break his heart, the I'd forgive him.

*Betty.* I've got it! oh, it will be such fun—oh, such fun!

*Mrs. S.* What is it, Betty, what is it? oh, do tell me?

*Betty.* Oh, ma'am, I can hardly do it for laughing. Why, you must—yes, you must first——

*Scumble.* (*Heard without,* R. D.) Laura, my darling, where are you?

*Betty.* How provoking! I must tell you presently; only say to him, you are going to see your mother at Hampstead—mmm!

*Enter* SCUMBLE, R. D., *in a blouse, a Greek cap on his head.*

*Scum.* Oh, there you are, my darling! Come, give your hubby a kiss. (*Kisses her.*)

*Mrs. S.* (*Aside.*) The hypocrite!

*Scum.* (*Aside.*) The pretty dear is at her window—I kissed my hand to her, she laughed at me, so I know she has had my letter.

*Mrs. S.* My dear, I hope you won't be cross, but I wish to go out to-day.

*Scum.* It's impossible! I cannot go out with you to-day—my picture there will never be finished for the exhibition. (*Gets on stool, begins to paint.*)

*Mrs. S.* No, dear, I don't want you to go at all. I'm merely going to see my mother, at Hampstead.

*Scum.* Why, my dear, you were there only last Wednesday. (*Aside.*) I hope she'll go!

*Mrs. S.* That's true; but mamma expected a letter from my brother, who has been abroad for so many years, and I—I——

*Betty.* (*Aside to Mrs. Scumble.*) Say you wish to remain all night.

*Mrs. S.* And I wish to remain all night.

*Scum.* Eh, all night? Oh, well, my dear, whatever you wish! But what's to become of me? I shall be miserable till your return. Who's to tuck me up at night?

*Mrs. S.* Oh, Betty will do everything for you!

*Betty.* (L.) Indeed, Betty won't, though.

*Mrs. S.* She shall get you a nice little dinner.

*Scum.* Dinner! no, no! When you are out, anything does for me—a slice of the cold shoulder of mutton we had yesterday will be quite enough; it's true it is not over done.

*Betty.* (*Aside.*) We can't say that of your hypocrisy.

*Mrs. S.* Then I have your permission?

*Scum.* I can refuse you nothing. But, mind,

muffle yourself up warm, and come back in the morning as early as you can. I want to give you a lesson.                          (*Goes to picture*, R. C.)

*Betty.* (*Aside.*) That's exactly what we want to give you!

*Mrs. S.* Come, Betty, you shall go and see me into the Hampstead omnibus—(*Aside*)—and tell me what I'm to do next.

*Betty.* Yes, ma'am.

*Scum.* What, going without one adieu? (*Mrs. Scumble returns, he leans down and kisses her.*) Excuse my getting off the stool.

*Betty.* (*Aside.*) It will prove a stool of repentance to you, or I'm much mistaken. Come, ma'am!

*Mrs. S.* Farewell, dear!

[*Exeunt Mrs. Scumble and Betty*, C. D. to L., *Scumble looks knowingly round to see that they are really gone, and exclaims—*

*Scum.* My wife's out! my wife's out! What a day of it I will have! (*Gets off the stool, and walks about much excited.*) What shall I do? Shall I go to Greenwich fair, and have a roll down the hill with the girls? Gracious, what an opportunity this would be to have my little French charmer from over the way—my model for Diana! Model, ha, ha! we artists are wicked dogs. Upon my soul, I'm almost too bad, I really am; but poor women are so simple, so weak, a child might deceive them. There's my poor wife has not a suspicion, bless her, and that simple soul, Betty, I really think she has no eyes at all—she never sees anything; she's a perfect fool, I can easily manage her. I will do it—I'll have Diana over, that I will. I'll have a nice little elegant repast, a bottle of champagne, and after dinner I'll have a waltz with her; the French are capital dancers. I'm very fond of dancing—it's so nice; the arm round the waist, her hands, the one reclining in your own, the other resting on your shoulder—eh, delightful!

(*Sings* "La, la, la, la," *and twists round.*)

*Enter* BETTY, C. D., *from* L.—*she comes down without seeing him, just as he stops twisting round he catches her in his arms.*

*Betty.* Law, master, are you mad?

*Scum.* (*Resting his head on her shoulder.*) Support me—I'm giddy!

*Betty.* You are very giddy indeed. Why, I thought you were going to be so very melancholy!

*Scum.* So I am melancholy, Betty, but different people have different ways of showing it—this is mine.

*Betty.* Master, do you know, I begin to think you are not much better than you should be, and I'm afraid you have been looking at the young woman opposite, as you sometimes look at me.

*Scum.* (*Winking.*) Do you, though?

*Betty.* Come, be quiet, now, or I won't tell you what I could tell you.

*Scum.* What is that, Betty?

*Betty.* That young Frenchwoman opposite is in love with you, she is. She beckoned me over as I came in, and gave me a sixpence and a note; the sixpence for you—no, the sixpence for me, and the note for you. Look here!           (*Shows note.*)

*Scum.* (*Aside.*) It's the answer to my letter. (*Aloud.*) Give it to me, there's a dear!

*Betty.* I'm not dear to you, for you never gives me nothing.

*Scum.* But I will—there's half a crown.

*Betty.* And here's the note; it does smell so nice, doesn't it? (*Pushes it against his nose.*) I suppose she calls it a Billy-dux.

*Scum.* (*Opens it.*) Why, it's all in French—never mind, I can read French. (*Reads—they both look over it at the same time.*) "Je vous aime, je vous adore—Je viendrai diner avec vous, a 5 heurs—Camille." You see I can read French, but unfortunately I can't understand it. I wonder where my dictionary is—I only took six Hamiltonian lessons.

*Betty.* And they didn't teach parley-wooing at the Sunday-school I went to, but let me try. There is one word I can make out, look—d-i-n, din, e-r, er, diner, and there's a figure of 5—I have it, I know I have—she means to come to dinner at five o'clock.

*Scum.* I've no doubt that's it. Now, Betty, Betty, Betty, Betty, you must befriend me; the truth is, I did write to her, but only just to ask her to come and sit as a model for my Diana. Somebody must sit.

*Betty.* Why wouldn't missus a done?

*Scum.* Nonsense, who ever heard of a married Diana? No, no, Diana was always a maid.

*Betty.* Then I should do, for I have been a maid ever since I was thirteen. But, I say, master, how is it you never have your lady models come when your wife is at home?

*Scum.* Quite accidental, I assure you! But now, dear Betty—(*Takes her round the waist*)—you must keep all this a secret, and provide a nice little repast, won't you—won't you, dear?

(*Kisses her.*)

*Betty.* (*Aside.*) Master's a nicer man than I thought he was. (*Aloud.*) But what would missus say, if she knew it?—there'd be a pretty rumpus.

*Scum.* I give you my honour, I won't tell her.

*Betty.* Well, then, I'll do it—but what will you have?—pork? I'm fond of tripe and onions.

*Scum.* You nasty beast! No, no, a nice little dinner of two or three covers. A nice duck, and then I can show off my wit, about sitting with a nice little duck at one end of the table—

*Betty.* And a little goose at the other.

(*She runs off*, C. *to* L.)

*Scum.* Admirable, admirable! poor simple thing, the kiss did it. I really feel that I can turn any woman round my little finger. But what am I to do, if my French beauty cannot speak English? but no matter. I have an eye, and I can talk with that to perfection. (*Gets on his stool, and paints.*) How I long for five o'clock. Now for Actæon's horns. (*Horn heard without.*) Ha, ha! that's very droll, just when I mentioned horns the signor begins to practice. He is always playing the same air, I suspect it's a signal to some one. I wish I had his whiskers, then I should be perfect. Oh, dear, how happy I do feel—my wife's out, and I'm all over of a flurry. My nerves are all of a—— (*A knock at* C. D.) What's that? (*Scumble starts, and nearly falls off the stool.*) How that knock agitated me—suppose it should be she! I'm all of a tremble—come in! Oh, I forgot she's French—outray, outry, ontry!

*Enter* AUGUSTUS DOBBS, C. D. *from* L., *his hair dressed à la German student.*

No, it's a gentleman.

*Dobbs.* I hope I have made no mistake. (*Looking at Scumble.*) No, there is no mistaking the diamond eye of genius; there it is. (*Points his finger at Scumble.*) There, I at once behold all that wonderful talent I had been led to expect, beaming in his visage. Oh, shades of Raphael, Correggio, Caraccia, there do you all stand embodied in one man and that man is——

*Scum.* (*Bowing.*) Mr. Scumble!

*Dobbs.* I knew it, I have not been misinformed.

*Scum.* You really flatter me too much; but may I ask to what I owe the honour?——

*Dobbs.* You may, and I will tell you. Know then, sir, that I require you, for once, to descend from your high throne of originality, and to become a copyist. (*Pulls him off the stool.*) I wish you to copy one of the greatest works of art, a miniature, which, taken as a work of art, transcends all other works of art; but, taken as a study from nature, it becomes divine.

*Scum.* You don't say so!

*Dobbs.* Are you capable of feeling the power of love?

*Scum.* Love! I live on it! I'm a perfect Cupid without wings.

*Dobbs.* Then you will feel for me. (*Crosses to* C.) Sir, I love, and am beloved by the angelic original of the miniature you shall presently behold. I want a confidant, a friend, will you be mine? I see you will—then I will unbosom myself.

*Scum.* (*Aside.*) I think he's a little mad.

*Dobbs.* You must swear secrecy, for know, I have the misfortune to be born a poet, like Petrarch.

*Scum.* Do you think that a misfortune?

*Dobbs.* Yes, for I love a Laura: and my Laura, like Petrarch's Laura, has a husband.

*Scum.* The devil she has! Oh, go on, there's nothing I am more *au fait* at than affairs of this sort. I'm a devil amongst the women myself—and husbands are such fools, such dolts, such——

*Dobbs.* Are you married?

*Scum.* Eh? oh, yes! but my wife's so different to other men's wives, she's a perfect Lucretia, a perfect dragon of virtue. Go on, I'm your friend.

*Dobbs.* Know, then, that it was only last Wednesday I first beheld her—yes, last Wednesday, on my way to Hampstead.

*Scum.* Hampstead?

*Dobbs.* Yes, an omnibus passed me, when, through the window, I beheld an angel.

*Scum.* An angel in an omnibus? How odd!

*Dobbs.* Our eyes met, and by that one glance our fates were scaled—we loved. In another minute I found myself alone with her in the omnibus.

*Scum.* Lucky dog!

*Dobbs.* She told me her simple tale. It appeared she was married to an ugly little man, like yourself—(*Scumble draws up*)—like yourself, an artist. She refused to tell *his* name, but said her own was Laura.

*Scum.* What day did you say?

*Dobbs.* Wednesday.

*Scum.* Going to Hampstead?

*Dobbs.* Yes; and until we could meet again, she allowed me to keep this miniature—look, look on the angel!

*Scum.* The devil! (*Aside.*) I never saw such a resemblance to my own wife. Hampstead! Wednesday! omnibus!

*Dobbs.* You seem struck! no wonder. Is it not the perfection of beauty? What eyes, what hair, what lips! (*Kisses it violently.*)

*Scum.* I wish he wouldn't do that. What shall I do?—shall I own what I fear? No; I shall cut such a ridiculous figure, after what I've said. I'll get possession of the picture!

*Dobbs.* Will you undertake the job?

*Scum.* I will. Give it to me!

*Dobbs.* I will bring it by-and-by. I'll go at once, get it measured for a gold case, and return with it at five o'clock.

*Scum.* No, no, not at five—not by any means at five—any other time. I shall be out then—I shall be out all the evening.

*Dobbs.* No matter; I can leave it with the servant. Adieu, my best friend!

(*Offers his hand.*)

*Scum.* (*Is about to take it, then draws back.*) Excuse me, I *never* shake hands.

*Dobbs.* Mind you keep my secret. I pity the poor devil of a husband, don't you?

*Scum.* I do, upon my soul! [*Exit Dobbs, C. to* L.] It can't be my wife—no, that's impossible! (*He seats himself musingly.*) Yet, it's very odd! Hampstead!—and he certainly said last Wednesday! No, no; I see it now—it *can't* be my wife! His lady said her husband was an *ugly* little man—that proves it can't mean me. It's merely an accidental coincidence—but if it should be? (*Looking at the large picture.*) I don't think I like the subject of my picture so much as I did. That figure of Actæon is not agreeable; it reminds one of—— (*Horn heard without.*) I wish that horn was stuffed down his throat! I shall give that fellow warning; curse me if he shall stay here!

*Enter* BETTY, C. *from* L.

*Betty.* Well, master, I have ordered such a nice little dinner from the French eating-house down the street; it will be here exactly at five o'clock. Law! you don't seem in spirits, Has anything happened?

*Scum.* Law, no, Betty! I was never in better spirits—la, la, la, la, la! (*Hums the tune of the horn.*) Curse that air!

*Betty.* That young French miss is in luck to get such a beautiful——

*Scum.* Don't flatter me so!

*Betty.* You—pooh! Such a beautiful dinner; for such nice things as I've ordered I'd sit for Weenus herself or any on 'em every day of my life. Where will you dine, master?

*Scum.* Oh, here, there, anywhere!

*Betty.* Then I may as well lay the cloth, for it's past four now.

*Scum.* Oh, is it? Then I had better go and adorn myself a little.

*Betty.* And just shave again, for your beard's uncommon rough.

*Scum.* A very good hint, Betty. You are quite right; when one is to be in *tête-à-tête* with a lady, always have a smooth chin. Let that will do for a maxim.

[*Exit Scum,* L. 4 E. R. D.

*Betty.* Oh, you're a wiseacre, you are! Ha, ha! poor simpleton! what vanity he must have to imagine he could deceive two such heads as mine and missus's. (*Goes to sideboard.*) Oh, here's the cloth! I don't think Mr. and Mrs. Scumble are very comfortable; but they try to cover it over. (*Throws cloth over table.*) To my mind, people are very foolish to get married. Whenever I see a couple going to church, I think—there's the spoons—(*Places spoons on table*)—if they'd only take my advice; but advice, to be good, must be seasonable. Pepper, salt, mustard. (*Puts them* on table.) Now, look at master! he'd be a very nice man, a very nice man, indeed; but then he has a wife—there's the vinegar.

(*Puts it on table.*)

*Enter* SCUMBLE, R. D., *finely dressed.*

*Scum.* I think that will do—eh, Betty? Look at me all round. (*Turns about.*) I wish you'd try if my chin's smooth now.

*Betty.* No, thank you, sir; once of such fun is quite enough.

*Scum.* But you shall! only just a little one. (*Catches hold of her; a loud double knock is heard.*)

*Betty.* That's your model, depend upon it.

*Scum.* If it be, take her into the other room first.
[*Exit Betty, C. to L.*
I feel quite nervous. I'll take a glass of wine to give me spirit.

*Enter* BETTY, C. *from* L.

*Betty.* Please, sir, here's another gentleman what wants his face painted or summat.

*Enter* MRS. SCUMBLE, C. *from* L.—*She wears a Chesterfield coat, buttoned up, a travelling cap, carries a neat cane, and altogether has the appearance of a young officer out of uniform.*

*Mrs. S.* (C.) You are the celebrated artist, Mr. Scumble—don't talk, I know it! (*Turning to Betty.*) And what is your name, my pretty wench?

*Betty.* (L.) Betty, at your service.

*Mrs. S.* Betty! Ah, your name is not so pretty as your face; therefore, I shall always address you by face, and not by name. (*Kisses her.*) Take that, my darling!

*Scum.* But, sir, I——

*Mrs. S.* Don't talk! I'm a young officer in Her Majesty's service, and am in that position that young officers very often are!

*Scum.* In debt?

*Mrs. S.* No, sir, in love! In love to distraction! madness! desperation! Now, Mr. Scumble, we military men are men of few words—

*Scum.* (*Aside.*) It doesn't seem like it.

*Mrs. S.* And, as I told you before, I am in love; but you will feel for my misery when I state to you, that she is the wife of another! Would I knew him—I'd cut his throat. (*Crosses* R.)

*Scum.* Bless my heart, you don't say so?

*Mrs. S.* Don't talk, I tell you. Had she been single, she would not have been married.

*Betty.* (—. Good gracious!

*Scum.* That's true!

*Mrs. S.* And I should have been happy!
(*Stands for a moment absorbed.*)

*Betty.* Master, now's your time; you can get a word in now.

*Scum.* Sir!

*Mrs. S.* (*Suddenly turning.*) Sir!

*Scum.* (*Starting.*) I was only going to ask of what service I can be?

*Mrs. S.* Can you paint miniatures?

*Scum.* I should rather think I could, when they are well paid for.

*Mrs. S.* Paid for! You shall have a mine of wealth if you do the original but half the justice she deserves. I've only just left her. She has told her fool of a husband she was going to Hampstead to see her mother. Ha, ha, ha!

*Betty.* Ha, ha, ha!

*Scum.* Betty, leave the room!

*Betty.* Ho!
[*Exit Betty, L. door.*

*Mrs. S.* Wasn't it good?

*Scum.* Excellent!

*Mrs. S.* Are you married?

*Scum.* I? oh—why—yes, I may say I am.

*Mrs. S.* Then take my advice; always open your eyes when your wife wants to go alone to see her mother. There's a bit of advice for you. Well, we met, as we often had before, in the Hampstead omnibus, and walking over to The Three Spaniards, I thought as I saw her smiling beneath her white bonnet—

*Scum.* Did you say white bonnet?

*Mrs. S.* And in her dove-coloured pelisse—

*Scum.* You don't mean dove-coloured pelisse?

*Mrs. S.* I say, I thought I never beheld so lovely a figure. Oh, Laura, Laura!

*Scum.* Just say that name again.

*Mrs. S.* Laura! is it not a sweet name? But had you seen her yourself——

*Scum.* (*Aside.*) I'm afraid I have, pretty often.

*Mrs. S.* You may imagine how she loves me when she, only this very day, gave me this diamond ring.

*Scum.* (*Aside.*) I shall fall; my own present to my own wife!

*Mrs. S.* If I could only find out who her husband was, I'd pick a quarrel with him, blow out his brains, and marry his widow.

*Scum.* (*Aside.*) Thank you. (*Aloud.*) But don't you think she must be a vile creature?

*Mrs. S.* The poor thing has her excuses. (*Pointedly to Scumble.*) She says she never thought of doing wrong, until she discovered that her own husband was making himself a fool with other women. You are married, Scumble; now if you would keep your wife good, be good yourself. Come, there's another bit of advice for you. I want to bring her here!

*Scum.* The devil you do!

*Mrs. S.* Yes, for you to paint her likeness.

*Scum.* If you do bring her here, I promise to paint her, and in her true colours, too.

*Mrs. S.* Thanks; and your reward shall be——
(*Horn heard without.*)

*Scum.* Curse that fellow!

BETTY *appears at* L. *door.*

Betty, go and tell the signor I'm not well, and that he must not play any more to-day. He shan't stay here!

*Betty.* They want to know if you are ready for the dinner to be sent in?

*Mrs. S.* Dinner, dinner! five's rather early. Now, my dear fellow, don't press me to stay, for I'm half inclined. Well, well, I see you wish it, therefore I will take a friendly snack with you.

*Scum.* But I don't wish it! it's impossible. I'm engaged; I've a great deal to do—I must be alone.

*Mrs. S.* Alone! why, the table is laid for two!

*Scum.* Betty, go and tell them I'm not ready for dinner yet.

(*As Betty goes out, she stumbles against* AUGUSTUS DOBBS, *who enters in a hurry, C. from* L.—*he has a cane.*)

*Betty.* Well, you're werry polite.
[*Exit C. to L.*

*Dobbs.* (*To Scumble.*) Oh, you are at home! how fortunate. There's the miniature; and only think of my happiness, I have seen her again. She was sitting waiting at the pastry-cook's just round the corner, eating a sausage roll.

*Mrs. S.* (R.) What's that, sir? Who are you speaking of in a pastry-cook's shop, eating a sausage-roll?

*Dobbs.* Who, sir? What business is that of your's.

*Mrs S.* But I imagine it is, sir.

*Dobbs.* Then know, sir, it was my own—my dear, dear, Laura.

*Mrs. S.* What sort of a person is she, sir? White bonnet, dove-coloured pelisse?

*Dobbs.* The same, sir, and that is her miniature.

*Mrs. S.* Why, that's my charmer.

*Dobbs.* No, sir, she loves none but me.

*Mrs.S.* It's false, sir, false!

*Dobbs.* Give me the lie, sir! take that.

(*Each strike at the other with their canes, but all the blows fall upon Scumble, who is between them.*)

*Scum.* Come, sir, I won't stand this!

(*Seizing his resting-stick—they all fight.*)

*Enter* BETTY, *screaming* C., *from* L.

*Betty.* What's the matter? Master, knock 'em both down, or you'll be murdered.

(*Pins down both his arms.*)

*Scum.* How the devil can I, if you hold my arms?

(*Shakes her off—Betty goes and holds back Mrs. Scumble—Scumble gets before Dobbs.*)

*Mrs. S.* This shall be answered for, sir. Yes, sir, you may depend upon it, this shall be answered for. There, sir, there is my card.

(*Gives card to Dobbs.*)

*Dobbs.* Oh, certainly, sir, the smell of powder won't make me faint: there is mine, sir!

(*Gives his card.*)

*Mrs. S.* You shall hear from me, depend upon it. Good-bye, old fellow, I haven't done with you yet.

[*Exit* C. *to* L., *in a great rage.*

*Scum.* I hope they'll kill each other. But, sir, I can stand this no longer, and I must say—yes, sir, I must say——

*Dobbs.* Hey-dey, what business is it of yours?

*Scum.* It is my business, sir, and I must confess——

*Dobbs.* Now, I want none of your confessions, all I want is for you to copy that miniature, and leave my concerns to me. I'll settle his business.

[*Exit.* C. *to* L.

*Scum.* Yes, and mine too, I'm afraid. Upon my life, this is pleasant: two fellows fight about your wife, and you come in for all the knocks. I say, Betty, what do you think of what you have heard?

*Betty.* I think it looks uncommonly queer. How has missus behaved to you lately?

*Scum.* Kinder than ever.

*Betty.* That looks very bad, for when a wife is kind to her husband, there must be something wrong—it's so unnatural.

*Scum.* But then I'm not *quite* sure it is Mrs. Scumble; in fact I won't believe it, until I have seen her, and taxed her with it—deuce take it, I'm forgetting my Diana all this time, and these fellows have so disarranged me, I'll just go and put myself a little in order, and do you finish the table.

[*Exit,* R. D.

*Betty.* Oh, yes, there's always something for Betty to do. I think the life of a maid of all work is worse than a nigger's; I'm getting heartily tired of it. (*Places things from sideboard on table.*) I wish somebody would marry me, and make me a missus. I'm falling away to a skeleton, I've such a deal to do.

SONG.

First early in the morning,
I rise soon after four,
I cleans my face, I cleans my boots,
And then I cleans the door.
At eight o'clock the milkman rings,
And chats a bit with me;
And then I makes the water boil,
And then I makes the tea.
　Now, there's a pretty life to lead,
　I swear, what oft I've said,
　I'll wed, and be a missus,
　For I won't remain a maid.
　No, that I won't.

At nine o'clock my missus rings,
And then begins to scold,
Because she's overslept herself,
Or 'cause the muffin's cold.
The dinner next I have to dress,
And then to dress poor me,
That I may look respectable
As I hands round the tea.
　Now, there's a pretty life to lead,
　I swear, what oft I've said,
　I'll wed, and be a missus,
　For I won't remain a maid.
　No, that I won't.

The evening, too, is not my own,
Then stockings I've to mend,
The comfort is, the longest day
At last comes to an end.
I go to bed, and think of John,
And sigh, and moan, and weep,
And then I think of John again,
And then I falls to sleep.
　Now, there's a pretty life to lead,
　I swear, what oft I've said,
　I'll wed and be a missus,
　For I won't remain a maid.
　No, that I won't.

[*Exit* C. *to* L.

*Enter* SCUMBLE, R. D., *as the clock strikes five.*

*Scum.* Bless me there's five o'clock, I don't feel half so loving as I did. It was certainly her ring that young fellow had—there couldn't be two so exactly alike—and then, that miniature! such a likeness! but I never knew she had a miniature.

*Enter* BETTY, C. *from* L.

*Betty.* She's come!

*Scum.* You don't say so! Well I must endeavour to banish all my fears and be as amiable as I can. Where is she?

*Betty.* In the next room, as you ordered.

*Scum.* There, now run and tell them to bring the dinner.

[*Exit Betty,* C. *to* L.

How provoking they should put me so out of spirits. I'll take a glass of wine to give me courage. Scumble, Scumble, be a man, and exert all your usual fascinations. Where are you, my darling dear, my dove, my duck? (*As he goes up to* R. *door, he sings*) "Ma chère amie," let me behold you. Fly to these arms.

*Enter* MRS. SCUMBLE, C. D. *from* L., *dressed as at first.*

*Mrs. S.* Ducky, dear!

*Scum.* (*Starting*) Eh, you here? I thought you were at Hampstead.

*Mrs. S.* No. Remembering this was your birthday, it seemed unkind to be away; so, after getting into the omnibus——

*Scum.* Then you have been in the omnibus?

*Mrs. S.* Why, you don't think I could *walk* to Hampstead, do you?

*Scum.* Who else was inside?

*Mrs. S.* Eh? Oh, why, only an old lady!

*Scum.* (*Quickly.*) In a Chesterfield coat, boots, and brass spurs?

*Mrs. S.* Mr. Scumble, are you deranged?

*Scum.* (*Aside.*) She does not appear much confused. I have it! that will settle all my doubts. (*Aloud.*) My dear, talking of birthdays, do you remember what I gave you on yours?

*Mrs. S.* To be sure I do, dear; it was a diamond ring—I always wear it.

*Scum.* Now, do you? Have you got it on now?

*Mrs. S.* See! (*Taking off her glove.*) Oh, gracious! where is it? I would not lose it for worlds. Oh dear! oh dear! what can have become of it?

*Scum.* False woman, you know well enough; but find it, find it! "That ring did an Egyptian to my mother give." It is more charmed than Othello's handkerchief; and if you have made away with it——

*Mrs. S.* You alarm me; but I shall find it—I shall find it!

*Scum.* No, no, you will never find that again; you gave it to——

*Mrs. S.* Ha, ha! now I remember, here it is in my reticule; look, darling! (*Shows it to him.*)

*Scum.* (*Astonished.*) Upon my life, so it is! Oh, my dear, come to my arms; you have taken such a load off my head, let me embrace you once more!

(*They embrace again.*)

*Enter* BETTY, R. D.—*she gets* L. *and points to* R. D. —*as they embrace, supposing the bonnet-maker to be there.*

I am so happy! (*Starts suddenly from her, as if remembering something.*) Gracious powers! I had forgotten all about the little French bonnet-maker. What am I to do with her? If she's found, I'm lost. (*Calling.*) Betty, Betty! here, Betty!

*Betty.* Yes, sir.

*Mrs. S.* No, I'll take my bonnet and shawl into the next room myself. (*Going towards* N. D.)

*Scum.* (*Places himself before her.*) No, no, my dear, not for the world—let Betty do it. (*Aside to Betty, in a voice made deep by agitation.*) And for heaven's sake get her out of the house, and stop the dinner!

*Betty.* Mum!

[*Exit* R, *with shawl.*

*Mrs. S.* I am so delighted I am in time, for I see you have not yet dined; I was determined to be here by *five.*

*Scum.* You will get a very poor dinner here to-day.

*Enter* WAITERS, *bringing in smoking dishes, &c. from* L.—*they place them on table.*

*Waiter.* Here is the dinner, sir!

[*Exeunt, C. to* L.

*Mrs. S.* Why, my dear, what is all this? A regular banquet, I declare! And—what do I see? The table is laid for two!

*Scum.* For two! Law, so it is!

*Mrs. S.* What does all this mean, Mr. Scumble?

You have been inviting company—and while I was out, too, Mr. Scumble.

*Scum.* Why, why, why, my dear, the truth is, I have had a young nobleman here, giving me some extensive commissions; and he, being alone in town, I—I—I asked him to dine with me at five. (*Aside.*) How provoking! I told him *not* to come.

*Mrs. S.* He is not very punctual.

*Scum.* Perhaps he has forgotten it, and will not come—it's more than likely.

*Enter* DOBBS, C. *from* L.

*Dobbs.* I beg pardon for popping in just at five, when I was told *not* to come at that hour, but——

*Scum.* You mistake—I told you to come. (*Winks.*) The dinner is quite ready. (*Aside to Dobbs.*) Say you came to dinner.

*Dobbs.* (*Aside to him.*) But why?

*Scum.* Never mind—say so!

*Dobbs.* But you've a lady there.

*Scum.* It's my wife. I've said you are a nobleman. (*Aloud.*) My dear, allow me to introduce you to Lord—(*Aside*)—what's your name?

*Dobbs.* Dobbs!

*Scum.* Lord Dobbs.

*Mrs. S.* A friend of yours.

(*They start—she makes signs.*)

*Scum.* They both started! She's making signs to him not to know her! (*Aloud.*) Have you ever met before?

*Dobbs.* Never!

*Mrs. S.* Never!

*Both.* Never!

*Dobbs.* (*To Mrs. Scumble.*) May I have the honour to hand you to the table? (*Takes her hand.*)

*Scum.* He squeezed her hand—I'll swear he did.

*Mrs. S.* Betty!

*Enter* BETTY, R. D.

*Betty.* Yes, ma'am!

*Mrs. S.* Another spoon. (*Calling to* Scumble.) Won't you come, dear?

*Betty.* (*To Scumble.*) She says she won't go until she has seen you or missus.

*Mrs. S.* My dear, his lordship is waiting.

*Scum.* I'm coming, my dear.

*Betty.* (*To Scumble.*) What am I to do with her?

*Scum.* Smother her.

*Betty.* Yes, sir.

[*Exit* R. D.

(*Scumble seats himself behind the table, Mrs. Scumble at the* R. *and Dobbs at the* L.)

*Dobbs.* It has often struck me that artists, without knowing it, in painting the human face, give a strong resemblance to themselves. Now, for instance, look at that figure of Actæon—do but notice how much that head is like Scumble's.

*Mrs. S.* I have thought so myself.

*Scum.* Have you, indeed?

*Dobbs.* Do you know, madam, while I sit here gazing in admiration on your lovely countenance, I feel I have beheld those features before.

*Scum.* Oh, it's the miniature—the likeness struck me directly.

*Dobbs.* The miniature! a daub—not worthy to be named in the same breath. No, no, Mrs. Scumble's lovely face is far more beautiful.

*Mrs. S.* Oh, sir!

*Dobbs.* Look at those eyes.

*Mrs. S.* You flatter!

*Dobbs.* Those lips—those teeth!

*Scum.* Don't grin, my dear.

*Dobbs.* You are a lucky dog, Scumble. Dear me,

here's the wishing bone. May I ask those delicate fingers to break it with me?

*Scum.* If he don't mind, my delicate fingers will break his head.

*Mrs. S.* Oh, sir, you are so gallant, I can refuse you nothing.

*Scum.* He's trying to touch her foot under the table, but I'll stop him. (*Pokes his foot about, at last he touches that of Dob's, who stamps furiously upon it.*) Oh, my corn! (*Jumps up and hops about with pain.*)

*Mrs. S. and Dobbs.* What's the matter—what's the matter?

*Scum.* Oh, nothing—only I had a sudden cramp in my foot. (*Aside.*) That fellow treads like a bullock.

*Mrs. S.* My dear Mr. Scumble, you don't seem to enjoy your dinner.

*Scum.* And can you wonder, madam, at that, when I behold the looks of affectionate intimacy with which that gentleman and you regard each other—you—Lord Dobbs?

*Mrs. S.* Nay, then, 'tis useless to dissemble further. (*Dobbs, n.*) I feel bewildered—delirious—delighted! Mr. Scumble, I must throw myself on your generosity, and confess all. You will think me mad, but——

*Scum.* But what?'

*Mrs. S.* I love that young man.

*Scum.* Horror!

*Mrs. S.* And my feelings are wrought up to such a pitch at this moment, that I cannot resist flying into his arms. Augustus, Augustus, do you love me!

*Dobbs.* (*Crosses to c, pushing Scumble over.*) Laura, Laura, Laura, I do!

(*They embrace.*)

*Scum.* Murder! robbery! fire! damnation!

*Enter* BETTY, R. D.

*Betty.* Murder! robbery! fire! da——
 (*Scumble stops her mouth with his hand.*)

*Scum.* Do you see that woman in that man's arms?

*Betty.* Yes, and what of that?

*Scum.* What of that? why, is not that my wife?

*Betty.* To be sure it is!

*Scum.* And who is that man?

*Betty.* That man? why, her brother!

*Mrs. S.* }
*Dobbs.* } Ha, ha, ha!
*Betty.* }

*Scum.* Her brother! Mr. A. Dobbs! Ha, ha, ha! Yes, yes, this is all very well; but there's another fellow in the question. What the devil's become of that military chap? he's not your brother.

*Mrs. S.* "Don't talk! we military men are men of few words." Ha, ha! you have been sadly cheated, and rightly served. I have forgiven you, and, if you behave well, will never do so any more.

*Betty.* Oh, master, I forgot, there's the little French bonnet-maker——

*Scum.* Hold your tongue.

*Betty.* (*Bawling*) There's the little French bonnet-maker——

*Scum.* Be quiet, you fool!

*Betty.* The little French bonnet-maker has eloped with Signor Cornuto, our second-floor lodger.

*Scum.* No, has she though? then joy go with them, though he does owe me three quarters' rent. Has he left nothing behind?

*Betty.* Not even his horns.

*Scum.* Ha, ha! I can afford to laugh at them now, though I confess they have caused me some disagreeable sensations in the course of the last few hours. However, I trust that my day's adventures may serve as a lesson to my married friends, and teach them, for fear of a checkmate, to restrain their roving propensities when their wives are out.

CURTAIN.

*Disposition of the Characters at the fall of the Curtain.*

| BETTY | DOBBS. | SCUMBLE | MRS SCUMBLE |
| R. | | | L. |

# BORROWING A HUSBAND;

## OR, SLEEPING OUT.

### A PETITE COMEDY, IN ONE ACT.

### BY WILLIAM T. MONCRIEFF.

*First Performed at the Royal Princess's Theatre, November 27th, 1843.*

## Dramatis Personæ.

[See page 21.

| | |
|---|---|
| Sir Vivian Delacourt ... ... ... | Mr. Walter Lacy. |
| Gilbert Buckhorn (Husband to Pamela) | Mr. Keeley. |
| Alec (Cousin to Pamela) ... ... ... | Mr. Oxberry. |
| Frisby (Confidential Valet to Sir Vivian) .. ... ... | Mr. Higgie. |
| John and Thomas (Servants to Sir Vivian)... ... ... | Messrs. Brown and Smith. |
| Dame Partington (Mother to Pamela) ... ... ... | Madame Sala. |
| Pamela (Wife to Gilbert and Cousin to Alec) .. ... ... | Mrs. Keeley. |

Scene.—Sir Vivian Delacourt's Country Seat in Somersetshire.

Time.—That of Representation.

Time of Representation.—One Hour and Fifteen Minutes.

# COSTUME.

---

The dresses are such as are usual for the respective Characters at the present period.

---

## STAGE DIRECTIONS.

EXITS AND ENTRANCES.—R. means *Right*; L. *Left*; D. F. *Door in Flat*; R. D. *Righ Door*; L. D. *Left Door*; S. E. *Second Entrance*; U. E. *Upper Entrance*; M. D. *Middle Door*; L. U. E. *Left Upper Entrance*; R. U. E. *Right Upper Entrance*; L. S. E. *Left Second Entrance*; P. S. *Prompt side*; O. P. *Opposite Prompt*.

RELATIVE POSITIONS.—R. means *Right*; L. *Left*; C. *Centre*; RC., *Right of Centre*; L.C. *Lef of Centre*.

R.        RC.        C        LC.        L.

\*₊\* *The Reader is supposed to be on the Stage, facing the Audience.*

# BORROWING A HUSBAND

SCENE I.—*Entrance Hall of Delacourt Manor House, an old Country Family Mansion of the Elizabethan period.*

*Enter* FRISBY, *picking his teeth.*

*Fris.* (*Foppishly.*) There, now all's right as a trivet, and the baronet can make himself scarce as soon as he likes. Not a very long visit, this of ours, to our old family mansion. How goes the enemy? (*Looking at his watch.*) Almost blindman's holiday—Sir Vivian will be here in the flashing of a pan—he's visiting his preserves—having a pop at the pheasants and partridges—they needn't be much afraid. Poor bipeds. Let me consider—I think I've settled all the requisites. Yes, the household are tipped—the bumpkins of tenants have had due notice to be regular with their rents—that the coin will always be acceptable—and——
*Sir Vivian* (*Without.*) Hallo! Frisby, Frisby!
*Fris.* Ah! a call of the house!—Sir Vivian!

*Enter* SIR VIVIAN, *through folding-doors in centre, as if from shooting—he throws himself into a chair—Frisby takes gun from him, which he has, terribly exhausted, trailed after him.*

*Sir V.* There, away with it, Frisby, that plaguy fowling-piece has nearly dragged my arm off. Shooting may be all very pleasant to those that are fond of it, but I can't say I'm one of the number, besides, I question its morality.
*Fris.* I hope you had good sport, sir!
*Sir V.* No, hang it! I saw plenty of game, Frisby' and the game saw plenty of me—rather too much, it should seem—for flying off, they left me to find out I'd been made game of myself—I never got a single shot. The dogs put up plenty of birds, but confound me if I could bring any of them down—at which those most sagacious quadrupeds seemed to be not a little astonished.
*Fris.* No doubt, sir, no doubt—but who would possibly take the trouble, I should like to know, to shoot game for themselves, now that they can buy as much as they like ready killed to their hands—it's only wasting powder and shot.
*Sir V.* Identically, Frisby—I declare I am quite tired of ruralizing—I'm glad I fixed to return to my parliamentary duties to-morrow—though this is my natal place, where I, Sir Vivian Delacourt, one of the lights of the land, passed my infant years. By-the-bye, have you been to Dame Partington, as I desired, Frisby?
*Fris.* I have, Sir Vivian, and have intimated your wish that she should wait on you this evening, with her daughter and son-in-law.
*Sir V.* 'Tis well—that's a duty must not be neglected. Morality, Frisby, morality—(*yawn*)—I

have not forgotten the good dame's daughter, the lovely Pamela—though but a mere boy when we originally met, I assure you I was by no means insensible to the charms of a pretty girl, sparkling eyes, a mouth of dewy rosebuds—she promised to be a perfect beauty, lovely, rapturous——
*Fris.* (*In an animated manner.*) And she has kept her word, Sir Vivian. Upon my reputation she is absolutely enchanting, exquisite—
*Sir V.* You have seen her, then, Frisby?
*Fris.* Yes, Sir V; I got a glimpse of the dear little creature as I looked in at the farm. A divinity in cotton, Sir V.—an angel in a straw hat—a fairy in pattens!
*Sir V.* (*Severely.*) Morality, Frisby, morality. I have a sacred duty to attend to—the last wishes of a beloved mother.
*Fris.* (*Rather abashed.*) Very true, Sir Vivian; identically, sir. The good old dame will, no doubt, soon be here.
*Sir V.* Did you see the husband? (*Yawning.*)
*Fris.* (*Also yawning.*) No—o—Sir Vivian, I suppose he was out when I called at the farm; but he'll come with them, for I told them you esteemed your character for morality so highly, that you could not possibly see the wife unless her husband came with her; but they'll all be here by-and-bye, no doubt; they know we start for our parliamentary duties the first thing to-morrow morning, and they won't give a chance away, trust them for that.
*Sir V.* Well, I'll just go and throw myself on the sofa for half an hour; you'll let me know the moment the little angel arrives, Frisby.
*Fris.* Identically, 'pon honour, Sir Vivian. [*Exit Sir Vivian.*] It's getting dark—these good individuals surely won't fail coming. From the old lady's self-satisfied air, when I delivered the message, I saw she guessed what it was for. (*Noise without.*) Eh! there's the outer gate opening—very likely our visitors. Yes, there's the pretty Pamela in 'propria—this way, this way, worthy persons. (*Running to open fold up doors.*)

*Enter* DAME PARTINGTON, PAMELA, *and* ALEC, *in their holiday clothes, shown in with much mock dignity by Frisby.*

*Dame.* (*Aside, encouragingly.*) Come along, child, come Alec, don't be afraid.
*Pam.* (*Timidly.*) I'm not afraid, mother.
*Dame.* (*Twigging Frisby, who is pulling up his frill.*) The Baronet's own gentleman—mustn't neglect him. (*Aside.*) Your servant, sir. (*Curtseying very low.*) Curtsey, child. (*To Pamela.*)
*Pam.* (*Curtseying in imitation of her mother.*) Yes, sir; your servant, sir, if you please, sir.
(*Aside.*) Gemini, what a fine man!

*Fris.* (*With supercilious nonchalance.*) Pretty little innocent, you are welcome, my dear!

*Dame.* We are come, as Sir Vivian desired, sir.

*Pam.* Yes, as Sir Vivian desired, if you please, sir. (*Curtseys, aside to Alec.*) Why don't you bow, Alec; how you stand there.

*Alec.* He, he, he! How do you do, sir; I hope you be very well?

(*Scraping rustically to Frisby, who is staring at him through eyeglass, and almost squeezing his hand off.*)

*Fris.* (*Rather ruffled, but recovering himself.*) The Baronet will be glad to see you, good folks; he has been expecting you. As it was getting rather late, I was half afraid you wouldn't come.

*Dame.* Oh, there was no fear of that, sir; we would not disobey Sir Vivian for the world.

*Pam.* No, not for the world, if you please, sir.

*Fris.* Disinterested sensibility! (*Aside.*) They know there is something to be got by it. (*Aloud,*) I will let the Baronet know you are here, my good individuals, directly. Sit down, and make yourself quite at home till I return.

*Dame.* (*Curtseying.*) I am sure you are very good, sir; I don't know how we shall ever thank you.

*Pam.* (*Curtseying.*) No, sir, we don't know how we shall ever thank you, sir.

*Fris.* (*Conceitedly, and with a patronising air, looking at Pamela.*) Not another word—Di Tanti Palpiti. [*Exit, humming opera air.*

*Alec.* He! he! he!—what a funny chap! Dry pantry—pan cakes. (*Imitating.*)

*Pam.* Dear heart, how beautiful everything is here! Look, Alec, only see what fine furniture; but I told you how grand everything was, you know—I used to be here almost every day, when I was a little girl, in poor dear Lady Delacourt's time. I'm almost afraid of sitting down.

(*Spreading out her clothes, and sitting down very gingerly.*)

*Alec.* It be carnation grandish, sartainly, cousin —beats playhouses all to nothing.

*Dame.* You remember what I told you, at the farm, Alec?

*Alec.* He! he! he!—to be sure I does. Why, lord, Dame, you repeated it over and over, to me, a hundred times—I be to pass off here as the husband of Pamela, and she's to be my wife. He! he! he!—I knows all about it.

*Dame.* Pamela, child—you know what you are to say to the Baronet?

*Pam.* Yes, mother—I'm to do everything to convince him that Alec and I are man and wife.

(*Alec sniggers.*)

*Dame.* His sending for us can only be to give us the fortune which your godmother, Lady Delacourt, always promised you should have, whenever you married, Pamela.

*Pam.* No doubt, mother; we mustn't lose that, it will be so handy in housekeeping, you know— and there's such a many things that we want.

*Dame.* The gentleman expressly said, you know, that we were to bring your husband, Gilbert, with us, Pamela, that the Baronet wanted particularly to see him. Now how could we do that when he's subpœnaed to Chipping Norton, in the Great Pig Cause—Grundy against Hogmore—and is not expected back for three or four days, which would be too late, as Sir Vivian sets off for London tomorrow morning. Great folks, you know, don't like to be disappointed.

*Pam.* I am sure it was the luckiest thing in the world that cousin Alec should pop in just as he did.

*Dame.* And the luckiest thought in the world that I should make him put on Gilbert's Sunday clothes, to come here in, and pass himself off for your husband.

*Alec.* Certainly, Dame—He! he! he! There be nothing I likes more than to be cousin Pamela's husband. (*Strutting about.*)

*Pam.* (*Dubitatingly.*) Surely there can be no harm in all this?

*Dame.* There can't, child—as soon as Sir Vivian sees us, he will give you the money, and away we go: so you see, Alec, you will not have to support your new character very long.

*Alec.* Oh, that will be no grievance. Dame— I shan't care how long I be Pamela's husband, for my part. He! he! he!

*Pam.* But I shall, though—and so will Gilbert.— I say, mother——

*Dame.* Well, child?

*Pam.* There's only one thing I'm afraid of in all this. It's very true we don't expect Gilbert back for three or four days, but he may come home tonight, you know, during our absence; then of course they'll tell him we are come to the Manor House, he'll follow, and find Alec here, and then— Oh, lord! oh, lord! you know how jealous he is.

*Alec.* Aye, aye, Cousin Pamela bean't so much out there—Gilbert would be ready to play the dickins wi' I, if he was to find I here, in his place—He! he! he!

*Dame.* He won't—he won't, no fear of that.

*Alec.* But there happens to be another little thing we've not thought of, Dame.

*Dame.* What, more misgivings? Well, let's hear what it is.

*Alec.* The Baronet will see I to-night as Pamela's husband—He! he! he! But suppose some other time he should happen to call at the farm, and see Gilbert there—why there might be an action for bigamy, or criminity conomy, or some pretty little thing like that—but I be quite agreeable—He! he! he!

*Dame.* You are a fool, Alec. No fear of his finding us out—I'll answer for that. Hush! here comes the Baronet's gentleman again.

(*All jump up and put chairs back.*)

*Enter* FRISBY.

*Fris.* Now, good people, I have informed the Baronet of your arrival, and he is prepared to see you—you will, therefore, follow me, and I will introduce you at once—Allons donc, mes amis.

*Alec.* He! he! he! Ding dong—that be French, or German, I reckon—jabbers like our old magpie.

*Pam.* (*Aside.*) Oh, how I tremble!—I'm afraid it's all very wrong.

*Dame.* (*Aside.*) Courage, child. (*Aloud.*) We are quite ready, sir.

*Fris.* This way.

*Alec.* Arter you, sir—He! he! he! Come Pamela—come Dame, heads up.

[*Exit Frisby, consequentially, after much ludicrous ceremony with Alec, who follows with Pamela and Dame.*

SCENE II.—*Antique Library in Delacourt Hall,* SIR VIVIAN *in rich morning gown, discovered lying negligently on a sofa, reading book.*

*Sir V.* Yes, the wishes of my dear mother performed, I will return to my parliamentary duties ; the interests of my constituents—my country— the obligations of filial affection—patriotism— morality—all.—Ah! here the little charmer comes.

*Enter* FRISBY, *conducting in* DAME, PAMELA, *and* ALEC, *the latter rather timidly, with a profusion of homespun bows and curtseys.*

*Fris.* Here are our rural friends, Sir Vivian.— That is the Baronet, my good people—Ya—aw! [*Retires, having introduced Pamela, &c.*

*Sir V.* Come forward, my good friends—don't be afraid.

(*Rises and advances to Pamela, whose hand he takes.*)

*Dame.* She bean't afraid, only a little dashed, your honour.

*Pam.* No, I'm not afraid, only a little bashed, your honour.

*Sir V.* You are welcome. (*Aside.*) Egad, she's very pretty! (*Regarding Pamela.*) Her rusticity is but the moss that enshrines the rose. (*Aloud.*) I am delighted to see you all. (*Alec smirks.*)

*Pam.* Your honour is very good, I'm sure, I'm very much obliged to your honour.

(*Curtseying confusedly*)

*Sir V.* (*Aside.*) She is perfectly irresistible. (*Aloud.*) Where's the happy man who has made himself master of so rare a work of nature?

*Alec.* He, he, he!—here I be, sir. He, he, he! I be the happy man. Bean't she a pretty one?

(*Chucking Pamela under the chin.*)

*Dame.* (*Aside.*) Booby! he'll spoil all. (*Secretly pulling Alec away.* *Aloud.*) Yes, that is my son-in-law, your honour. (*Alec making a scrape.*)

*Alec.* Yeas. How d'ye do, sir? He, he, he!

*Sir V.* (*Surprised.*) How! Pamela—is this your husband?

*Pam.* Ye—yes, your honour, this is my—my—husband, if you please, your honour!

*Alec.* He, he, he!

(*They look confusedly at each other.*)

*Dame.* He is very fond of Pamela, your honour.

*Alec.* Yes, main fond of Pamela, your honour—bean't I, Pamela? I loves her dearly. He, he, he!

(*Pamela makes signs to him, aside, discouraging his familiarities.*)

*Sir V.* (*To Pamela.*) I shall, with pleasure, give you the hundred pounds which I know my dear mother intended you to have.

*Dame.* A hundred pounds! Oh, your honour! u are really too good; I have got my pocket-book ready.

(*Taking out a large greasy black leather pocket-book.*)

*Sir V.* My steward shall hand you over the cash the very first thing, before you leave the Manor House, in the morning.

*Dame.* (*Frightened, aside.*) Oh, mercy! "the morning"—(*Aloud*)—to-morrow, your honour? Dear me—but we must go home to-night.

*Pam.* (*Alarmed.*) Oh, yes; we must go home to-night, if you please, your honour. (*Aside.*) Mercy on me! Gilbert would kill me if he knew I slept out all night.

*Sir V.* No, no—you must not think of going, it's getting quite dark. Your farm is more than five miles distant. You must pass the night here. There's every accommodation. It's all arranged.

*Pam.* (*Aside, much frightened.*) Oh, dear me, what shall we do?

(*Alec. Who has heard the arrangement with much satisfaction.*) I sees no objection, for my part, to staying here wi' Pamela all night. He, he, he!

*Dame.* I am very sorry, your honour, to refuse, but we must positively return home to-night.

*Sir V.* Nay, nay, my good dame. Hark! isn't that thunder? (*Thunder heard.*) Yes, it is a harvest storm. You can't go through the storm. You can't set off now. What say you, my pretty little Pamela? You are not in any particular hurry to leave me, surely.

*Pam.* Oh, yes—that is—no, your honour, I—the storm—certainly. If your honour insists—but—but—

*Alec.* We can't go through the storm. (*It begins to rain.*) His honour be right there, Dame.

*Dame.* Oh, certainly—provoking—but if we must —why—why—mercy on me.

*Sir V.* It's agreed on, then. We will all sup together. I have made up my mind to be Arcadian this evening—to unbend—to enjoy myself.—Little Pamela shall do the honours of the table, be the Sylvan Queen of the feast.

*Pam.* (*Curtseying.*) I'm sure I'm very much obliged to your honour.

*Alec.* (*Aside.*) And I'm sure I bees—He! he! he! (*Storm increases.*)

*Sir V.* Egad, it comes down rarely—it's well we are housed, friends—I shall join you in the refectory when supper is ready, of which you shall have due notice.

[*Exit Sir Vivian.*

*Dame.* (*Storm increases—Omnes look at each other frightened.*) We are in a pretty mess, now,—I'v. afraid we've done very wrong.

*Pam.* Yes, yes, very wrong indeed, mother. (*Thunder.*) Ha! Heaven preserve us.

(*With a slight scream, much frightened.*)

*Dame.* How unfortunate, the storm coming on.

*Pam.* Unfortunate, indeed, mother—but we might be sure there would be a storm, sleeping out without leave!

*Alec.* I don't see what harm there be—I can't say I be at all sorry, as far as I be concerned, that we be going to stay, for I ha' got a woundy appetite—he! he! he!

*Dame.* Well, since we are in for it, we must try and arrange matters the best way we can.

*Gilbert* (*Without.*) I'll find my way mysen—Sir Vivian will be glad to see I—so pray doan't trouble yoursel, gentlemen. In the liberary are they? Well, I'll go into the liberary, too.

*Pam.* (*Frightened.*) Oh, my gracious, what do I hear?

*Alec.* (*Looking off.*) Consarn it! if it bean't cousin Gilbert! Here'll be a carnation rumpus—he! he! he!

*Dame.* Gilbert! mercy on me—what will become of us? I hope he hasn't let the cat out of the bag. Lord bless me, how I tremble!

*Pam.* I shall die—I'm sure I shall—here he is!

*Enter* GILBERT.

*Gil.* Wheugh! what a soaking I ha' got, surely. (*Shaking the rain off him.*) Oh, here you all be—that's right—they said you were this way—I be main glad I ha' found you,

*Dame.* Mercy on us, who would have thought of seeing you here, Gilbert?

*Gil.* And who would have thought of seeing you here, Dame, if you com'st to that?

*Dame.* What did you say to the gentleman that let you in— and what brought you here?

*Pam.* Yes, what did you say to the servants, Gilbert?—and what brought you here?

*Gil.* Why my two legs brought I here, to be sure. The trial be put off. (*Dame groans.*) You needn't grant so, Dame—Hogmore be afeard, so in course I come back. When I got to the farm, I found you had set out for Manor House, here, wi' Alec and Pamela; so as what be good for goose be good for gander, I set off arter you—and nicely caught in the storm for my pains I ha' been, too.

*Pam.* I am sure you had much better have stopped where you were, Gilbert.

*Alec.* (*Quickly.*) Yes, you'd ha' much better ha' stopped where you were—I thought you wasn't to come back for these two or three days, Cousin Gilbert?

*Dame.* (*Much vexed.*) What a mess you've got us all in—who was it you asked for, when you came, tell us that?

*Pam.* Tell us that, Gilbert.

*Gil.* Why, I asked whether Dame Partington and her daughter were here, to be sure. Who would you have had I ask for?

*Dame.* (*Anxiously.*) And was that all you said?

*Pam.* (*Eagerly.*) Yes, was that all, Gilbert?

*Gil.* To be sure it wur—what a worrying you do keep.

*Dame.* Well, then, there's no particular harm done yet, and, to prevent any being done, you must be off again directly. (*Pushing him.*)

*Pam.* Yes, my dear Gilbert, you must be off directly, as fast as you possibly can.

(*Pushing him.*)

*Alec.* Yes, you mun be off directly, Cousin Gilbert, as fast as you can. (*Pushing him.*)

*Gil.* Off, directly, after I've got so woundy wet wi' coming up here! but I'll be danged if I will be off, though—I begin to smell a rat—there be summat iu the wind—but I don't care for that, I shu'n't budge a foot, that be flat, I'll not go without my wife.

*Omnes.* (*Severally.*) Your wife! hush! hush!

*Gil.* Why, beean't Pamela my wife? Warn't banns asked tu'ee times? What the Jickens be the matter wi' you all?—you look as scared as a March hare, pushing and shoving a body about, and all that nonsense.

*Dame.* Um! I see we must tell him all about it.

*Pam.* Yes, yes, mother—we must tell him all about it. You know what an obstinate animal he is.

*Gil.* So much the better, and I hope I may never be anything worse than an obstinate animal, wife. Well, tell us what this wonderful secret be.

*Dame.* Well, then, Gilbert, this is the long and the short of it. You must know that Alec passes off here for your wife's husband—for you!

*Gil.* (*Astounded.*) Eh?

*Dame.* Yes, his honour insisted on seeing Pamela's HUSBAND when he paid her her FORTUNE —he is going to London to-morrow. You were not expected home these three days—Alec happened to pop in—so, to secure the fortune we have brought him here to pass for you—he stands in your shoes.

*Gil.* Stand in my shoes! Yes, and ecod, he's got my best Sunday breeches on, too. (*Twigging them.*) I'll be danged if I can stand that!

*Alec.* Yes, but it be only till to-morrow morning, Cousin Gilbert—be! he! he!

*Gil.* Why, consarn it, that be worse than all— only till to-morrow morning, indeed!

*Pam.* (*Coaxingly.*) Yes, dear Gilbert, only till to-morrow morning—Sir Vivian insisted on it, and we could not possibly refuse him, you know.

*Dame.* What is there to object to, Gilbert?

*Gil.* What is there not to object to, if it comes to that? It be no use talking, Dame, you mun s; y what you like, but no one shall be Pamela's husband but mysen.

*Dame.* You'll get us all turned out of the house, we may then bid good-bye to the fortune—a hundred pounds!

*Gil.* (*Whistling.*) A hundred pounds!—carnation —mustu't lose that, that will never do. Well, I suppose I mun let you ha' your own away, as brass depends on it.

*Alec.* Hush! Here comes Baronet's gentleman. He! he! he!

*Pam.* My goodness! what shall we do?

*Dame.* There is but one way, Gilbert—as Alec passes off here for you, you must pass off here for Alec.

*Gil.* How! Be I to be my own cousin? Find a substitute for mysen, that be worse than militia. But no matter—I shan't be obliged to go away to-night, and that wur all I wanted. (*Aside.*)

### Enter FRISBY.

*Fris.* Now, then, good folks. Eh! this stranger! (*Seeing Gilbert.*) Oh, the new comer that Thomas was speaking about. Who's this, Dame?

*Dame.* Nobody, your honour.

*Pam.* No, nobody, if you please, sir.

*Alec.* No, he be nobody. He! he! he!

*Gil.* (*Bristling up.*) Carnation! I nobody!

*Fris.* (*Facetiously.*) Nobody! There isn't much of him, to be sure.

*Dame.* We mean, sir, it's only our Cousin Alec. Hearing we were here, he has taken the liberty of coming to pay his respects to his honour.

*Fris.* Oh, the cousin, eh?

*Gil.* Yes, sir; I be cousin's cousin. (*Scraping.*)

*Fris.* Well, my honest fellow, you shan't be disappointed. (*Slapping him on the leck*) I'm just come to let you know, good people, that you may repair to the Refectory as soon as you like. I shall inform Sir Vivian of this worthy person's arrival —for the present you'll excuse me. "Non piu audrai farfalloue Amoroso," &c.

[*Exit Frisby, humming opera air.*

*Gil.* (*Staring with stupid wonder.*) "Merry Andrew!—sarcy fellow!—hammer-who so?" what do he mean by that? There, it be all settled, you see, and I be to stay. Let's go to this Infeetory at once, Dame—(*Crosses to right with Dame*)—for I be plaguy sharp set. Come, Cousin Alec—come, Mistress Pamela. (*Aside.*) How glad I be trial wur put off, or, fegs! there mought ha' been another trial. Sleeping out don't so much matter —provided I sleeps out, too, and we be all under same roof, as it wur. (*Aloud.*) Come along.

*Dame.* (*Aside.*) Mercy on me!

*Alec.* (*Aside.*) I wish the pigs had been smothered before trial had been put off. Come, wife Pamela. He! he! he!

*Gil.* I say, Master Alec, none of that—mind what you are at there—consarn it

[*Exeunt Dame, Pamela, Gilbert, and Alec—Gilbert pulling Pamela away from Alec.*

SCENE III.—*Refectory of the Manor House, Supper Table discovered, laid out.*

*Enter* FRISBY, *conducting in* DAME, PAMELA, GILBERT, *and* ALEC.

*Fris.* This way, my good people—this is the Refectory, where you were to come. You will sup quite *comme il faut* here. The Baronet will join you in a twinkling. (*Calling off to Servants.*) Here John, Thomas, my good fellows—prepare the edibles, and get all ready, *toute suite.*

*Dame.* Dear heart, how grand; his honour is really too good.

*Fris.* (*Patronizingly.*) Not at all, not at all, old lady, we can't help it, it's our nature, la, la! (*Singing, and pulling up his shirt collar.*) Oh, here is Sir Vivian.

*Enter* SIR VIVIAN, *dressed for evening party.*

*Sir V.* So, my good friends, we have an addition to our party, I hear, our COUSIN—you must introduce me, Pamela.

*Pam.* (*Confused.*) Certainly, your honour—this —this is our Cousin Alec, if you please.

*Gil.* (*Aside.*) How ready the baggage be to cozen I, surely.

*Dame.* Yes, this is Cousin Alec, your honour.

*Gil.* (*Bowing and scraping.*) Servant, sir, my humble duty to you—hope I sees your honour quite well—proud and happy to pay my respects to your honour—Ahem !

*Dame.* There, that will do, Alec, that will do. Well, now then that you have seen his honour, and said what you had to say, you can make your bow and go back again.

*Gil.* (*Aside.*) Go back, and leave my Pamela ; that will never do—besides the waters be out, I shouldn't be able to get across fields.

*Sir V.* Go back, Dame!—by no means, I positively can't think of such a thing—Cousin Alec will do very well where he is.

*Gil.* (*Significantly.*) Yes, I shall do very well where I be.

*Sir V.* (*To Gilbert.*) You have no objection to stay and pick a bit of supper with us, have you, friend Alec?

*Gil.* Lord love 'ee, not a morsel, sir—I'll stay and pick supper wi' you, *above* a bit, sir, wi' all the pleasure in life ; anything to oblige your honour—I've a main good appetite.

*Sir V.* Ha ! ha !—well said, Cousin Alec, it's all settled, then—you'll be able to amuse us while we are at supper.

*Gil.* Oh, yes, I be main amusing. (*Aside.*) I can amuse him and mysen too. Won't I make beef look foolish, neither.

*Sir V.* Have you executed my orders, Frisby— are the apartments of my good friend, Mrs. Partington, and that of her son and daughter, duly prepared ?

*Fris.* All ready, Sir Vivian—the Dame will sleep in the Blue Chamber, and the young married couple in the Yellow Room—the beds are well aired —they are the only two apartments that are in use for sleeping rooms, now.

*Sir V.* That's unlucky, for we shall want a room for this honest fellow, our cousin.
(*Pointing to Gilbert, who has manifested much uneasiness at what he has heard.*)

*Fris.* Don't make yourself uneasy about him, Sir Vivian, there's the room in the summer-house, at the bottom of the garden, that Tom Arsenic, the rat catcher, sleeps in occasionally, when he visits these parts to physic the animals, it has been occupied very lately, and is well aired.

*Gil.* (*Aside, showing still greater dissatisfaction.*) The rat catcher! I be caught! Oh, lord !

*Fris.* Mr. Alec will find it very comfortable—and then he need be under no sort of fear, he'll be well taken care of, for he'll have the gardener's two dogs, Cæsar and Dragon, as his protectors for the night.

*Gil.* (*Aside, greatly frightened.*) Cæsar and Dragon ? Dickens ! what pleasant companions.

*Sir V.* That will do capitally—the very thing. Yes, yes, we couldn't be so cruel as to separate the newly-married couple.

*Gil.* (*Aside.*) Consarn it !

*Sir V.* I don't know what my friend Gilbert, here—(*Pointing to Alec*)—would say if we did.

*Gil.* (*Much disconcerted.*) Gilbert would say he didn't approve of married people being *separated*, sir. (*Pointedly.*)

*Sir V.* Suppose, Frisby, while supper's getting ready, you let our friends see their different apartments.

*Dame.* Your honour is very good, and Alec, here—(*Pointing to Gilbert*)—had better see where he is to sleep, too.

*Sir V.* Undoubtedly. Frisby, show our cousin to the summer-house ; take care of the dogs. I shall select the wines for supper, with Evans, the butler, myself, while you are gone.
[*Exit Sir Vivian.*

*Fris.* I'll take care, Sir Vivian. (*Calling off.*) Thomas, my good madam, will show you and the young couple your several bedrooms ;—(*Points to the left*)—while I convoy Mr. Alec, here, to the summer-house. (*Crosses to the right.*) This way. Follow me, my good friend.
[*Exit Frisby, humming air.*

*Gil.* I'm much obliged to you—— (*Stops on seeing Alec about to follow Pamela.*) I say, cousin, there be no occasion for you to be going wi' Pamela, you had better go wi' I, you understand— it will be more pleasant and proper, like—be a little walk for you.

*Alec.* Thank you kindly, consin ; but if it be all the same to you, I'd rather go wi' Pamela. He, he, he ! I don't want to walk just now. Besides, garden be damp, and it be so dark.

*Gil.* Consarn it—but I say——

*Dame.* Aye, aye. You had better go, Alec, if your consin, here, wishes it. (*Pushing Alec.*)

*Pam.* Yes, you had better go and keep consin Gilbert company. (*Pushing him.*) Come along, mother.
[*Exeunt Pamela and Dame.*

*Alec.* Umph ! gone—how glum Gilbert do look. (*Aside.*) If he don't like to go alone, I suppose I mun go wi' him—though I don't see what occasion there be—I be quite satisfied wi' his honour's arrangement. He be afeard of the dogs, I suppose. (*Aloud.*) Well, cousin, you shall ha' your own way.

*Gil.* (*Aside.*) Safe bind, safe find, they do say ; it be no use locking stable-door when steed be stolen. (*Aloud.*) I'll take your arm, cousin, wi' your leave.

*Re-enter* FRISBY.

*Fris.* Cousin Alec, an't you coming ?

*Gil.* Oh, yes; we be all ready now, sir. Cousin

*Gilbert*, here—(*Pointing to Alec*)—wishes to go wi' I, to make I *safe*, and I don't like to baulk him. (*Pointedly.*) You be sure dogs know you—better take your stick.

*Fris.* Don't be afraid, my friends, follow me.

[*Exeunt Frisby, Gilbert, and Alec, the two latter arm in arm, both unwillingly enough.*

*Re-enter SIR VIVIAN.*

*Sir V.* There, I've looked out the wines, no want of spirits. The simplicity of these honest rustics amuses me exceedingly—so unsophisticated—so natural; if anything could make me forget my parliamentary duties, I really think it would be that little gipsy Pamela. Yes, if I wasn't going to set off to-morrow, I wouldn't swear I mightn't fall in love with the baggage. That Gilbert is certainly a very happy rascal—I declare I almost envy the dog. It certainly is fortunate for all parties, saying nothing of morality, that I am going to London to-morrow.

*Re-enter PAMELA, not seeing Sir Vivian.*

*Pam.* Gracious goodness! how fine everything is, surely.

*Sir V.* (*Turning quickly.*) Why, here the little angel is. Is that you, my pretty Pamela?

*Pam.* (*Aside, confused.*) Sir Vivian here! mercy on me. (*Aloud.*) I beg your honour's pardon—I thought Alec and Gilbert had returned by this time.

*Sir V.* (*Taking her hand.*) No, we are alone, my charmer. Nay, you mustn't go away; I want to have a little conversation with you.

*Pam.* (*Timidly.*) With me, your honour? La, sir.

*Sir V.* Yes, you—you little rogue. I hope you are satisfied with the chamber I've provided for you?

*Pam.* I must be hard to please, if I wasn't, sir. It's only a great deal too grand and fine for simple folks like me and mother.

*Sir V.* Too grand, my dear—too fine! Nothing can be too grand and fine for such a little divinity as *you!* As for your mother, indeed——

*Pam.* Oh, sir, pray don't be angry—don't think I'm unthankful—but I don't know how it is, sir, yet somehow I seem to feel more at my ease in our little farm than I do in this grand mansion. I suppose it's because I haven't been born to it—it's not natural to me like.

*Sir V.* ——n to it! You were born to adorn any station, my love. How the plague do you manage to kill time in this same home of yours—that you were talking about?

*Pam.* Oh, your honour, I find as many things to do as the Queen herself would.

*Sir V.* Ah!

*Pam.* Yes, your honour. But I'll tell you——

*Sir V.* Yes, do tell me all about it.

*Pam.* Well, then, in the first place——

*Sir V.* Yes, in the first place——

*Pam.* In the first place, directly I get up, I feed the poultry, the cocks and hens, and the ducks, attend to the pigs, look after the dairy, milk the cows, set the cream, make the cakes for breakfast, put a rasher on the coals.

*Sir V.* And help to eat it—eh?

*Pam.* Oh, yes; that of course, your honour.

*Sir V.* Exquisite simplicity! Well?

*Pam.* Then I put the farm to rights, ride the pony, go to market, sell the eggs, return, mix the hog puddings, churn the butter, get dinner ready——

*Sir V.* And, of course, help to eat that too?

*Pam.* Oh, of course, sir—especially if it's something nice.

*Sir V.* Charming! Well?

*Pam.* Then I dress for the afternoon, sit down to my work, darn the stockings, mend the clothes till tea time; after tea, I sometimes visit a neighbour, or sometimes a few neighbours visit I; and wind up all, your honour, with forfeits, blindman's buff, roasted chestnuts, gooseberry wine, and sometimes a dance on the green, and kiss in the ring.

*Sir V.* Delightful! delightful! Ah, I see I don't know half the good things there are in the world. Why cannot I have hog puddings, gooseberry wine, and such a dear little enchanting, transporting, captivating——

*Pam.* La! your honour!

*Sir V.* You are all innocence, all rapture. Nature's own rose! Seducing, entrancing, delicious—I must kiss the dew from those pouting lips, you rogue, I must.

*Pam.* Oh, mercy! your honour!

(*As Sir Vivian is kissing Pamela, GILBERT enters hastily, and sees him, draws back in consternation.*)

*Gil.* (*Aside.*) Eh! carnation! Baronet smouching up my Pamela! Oh, dang it, this will never do—Ahem!—Ahem! (*Aloud.*)

*Sir V.* (*Aside, turning round.*) Hallo, the consin. Confound it, I'm forgetting my morality! but then she's the wife of one of my constituents, and parliamentary duty—plaguy *mal apropos* this interruption though. (*Aloud.*) Cousin Alec, so soon returned! I hope you like your room, snug and out of the way, isn't it?

*Gil.* Very sir, main snug. (*Aside.*) It be rather too much out of the way for my liking. (*Aloud.*) I can't say but I'd as leave be without the company of those two great dogs, though—they may be getting rather too fond of a body.

*Sir V.* Ha, ha, ha! the members for Barking, Cæsar and Dragon, they won't forget their duties, never fear; you'll soon get used to one another; they don't know you yet: you'll like them well enough when you are better acquainted.

*Gil.* Mayhap—mayhap.

*Pam.* (*Aside.*) Poor Gilbert—what a way he is in—I declare I am almost sorry for him.

*Enter DAME, in grand tenue.*

*Dame.* I hope I haven't kept your honour waiting, but I couldn't sit down with your honour till I had smartened myself up a bit, and I am not so nimble as I was forty years since.

*Sir V.* No apologies, I beg, Mrs. Partington—my good madam, all is free and easy here.

*Gil.* So it would seem, egad! (*Aside.*)

*Sir V.* You are quite in time, Dame, our cousin Alec is only just before you.

*Enter ALEC and FRISBY.*

*Alec.* Why, cousin, how you disappeared all of a sudden—he, he, he!

*Sir V.* Well, now as we are all here, and our friends must be wanting some refreshment, let supper be served up immediately, Frisby.

**Fris.** Directly, Sir Vivian.

*(Retires to side of scene and beckons on John and Thomas, who enter with supper—Frisby arranges table, under the direction of Sir Vivian, while they place chairs.)*

**Dame.** (*In a low tone to Gilbert.*) You see every thing be quite right, Gilbert, so you need not look so glum.

**Gil.** (*In a low tone.*) Right, indeed; I don't think every thing be quite so right, Dame—you haven't seen what I ha' seed just now.

**Dame.** (*Aside to Gilbert.*) Well, well, to-morrow will soon come, and then all will be over.

**Gil.** To-morrow! yes, but there be to-night. How be we to get over that? You don't catch I sleeping wi' dogs, when there be Pamela, I can tell thee that. If it warn't for fear of losing the hundred pounds——

**Fris.** (*Coming forward.*) Now, then, my good people, all's ready.

(*To Pamela, Dame, &c.—Servants bring table down.*)

**Sir V.** (*Also coming forward.*) Come friends, let us sit down and enjoy ourselves, take your places; you, Pamela, sit this side next to me—you, Dame, sit on the other. (*He sits down between Pamela and Dame—to Alec.*) You, Gilbert, sit next your wife. (*Alec takes seat next to Pamela.*) Ah, that's right—and you, Cousin Alec—(*To Gilbert*)—next to Dame Partington.

**Gil.** (*Aside.*) So, I be to be fobbed off wi' Dame, be I, very pratty—It ha' quite taken away edge of my appetite—carnation, how that fellow, Alec, be ogling my Pamela! I be sure I shan't be able to stand it out much longer.

**Dame** (*To Gilbert.*) Don't you hear what Sir Vivian says, Alec? you are to sit by me.

**Gil.** (*Sitting down sullenly.*) I heard what Baronet said, fast enough—Dame—I bean't deaf—(*Aside*)—nor dumb neither, as they mayhap may find out by-and-by.

**Sir V.** Charming Pamela, what say you to a wing of a chicken?

**Pam.** (*Aside.*) Oh, dear me, I wish I had a pair, and could fly away.

**Sir V.** Or a little bit of pigeon pie—there's a breast—(*Helping Pamela*)—you'll find it very tender. Friend Gilbert—(*To Alec*)—shall I help you to a merry thought?

**Alec.** Thank you, kindly, Baronet—who knows but I may ha' my wish, your honour—He, he, he!

**Gil.** (*Aside, very uneasily.*) His wish! I wish, wi' all my heart, it may choke him.

**Sir V.** (*To Gilbert.*) Honest Alec, you'll want something more substantial, perhaps you'd like a little of the cold mutton? help yourself.

**Gil.** (*Aside.*) Much obliged, sir, I won't be fobbed off wi' only cold mutton, I'll ha' some of pigeon pie, as well.

(*Helps himself plentifully, and eats voraciously.*)

**Sir V.** (*To Alec.*) Friend Gilbert, what say you to hob and nob in a glass of Madeira—Pamela will join us.

**Gil.** (*Almost choking himself while they fill—aside.*) I don't half like this hobbing and nobbing in Mydearee.

**Sir V.** We'll make it general—a glass all round —and I'll give you a toast. (*Filling glasses.*) Here's Courtship after Marriage!

**Omnes.** (*All drinking, except Gilbert.*) Courtship after Marriage!

**Gil.** I don't like folks courting after marriage—for my part.

**Sir V.** What, then, you are married, Cousin Alec?

**Gil.** Why, I doan't know if I be; I wur once, but I bean't now exactly—they've been unmarrying me!

**Sir V.** What! Oh, you are a widower, eh?

**Gil.** Yees I be, almost, your honour. I'm sure I might quite as well be one.

**Sir V.** Almost! how, almost? A very strange fellow, this.

**Pam.** He's a little dashed like, because—because he's on the point of being very soon re-married, your honour!

**Sir V.** Ha! ha! ha! Very good—no doubt your intended returns your affections, Cousin Alec?

(*To Gilbert.*)

**Pam.** (*Pointedly.*) She thinks he is a little too jealous, your honour.

**Sir V.** Jealous! Oh, fie! you must get the better of that, cousin Alec. Our friend Gilbert here—(*Pointing to Alec*)—don't seem at all jealous —you see how much at ease he is.

**Alec.** He! he! he! Yes; I be quite at my ease, sir. I knows Pamela's love for me.

(*Leers at her.*)

**Gil.** (*Aside, upsetting his plate and breaking it.*) Darn his impudence!

**Sir V.** Eh! what's the matter, friend Alec? Oh, only a plate broken! Never mind; accidents will happen in the best regulated families. Suppose we have a little harmony, as things seem somewhat discomposed, to restore good humour again? What say you, my little Pamela, to giving us a song—one of your real old English country ditties? It will be a novelty to me.

**Alec.** I seconds that, wi' all my heart. She knows plenty, your honour; she can sing a dozen if she likes—"The Cuckoo," "The Early Horn," "My Friend and Pitcher," "If a Body Kiss a Body"——

**Gil.** (*Aside.*) Oh, dang it, I shall go mad! Curse all horns and cuckoos, and kissing bodies!

**Pam.** (*Frowning on Alec.*) How can you tell such stories? Don't believe him, your honour; he only says so to vex me. He knows that I never sing—that I've no voice.

**Alec.** She be only bashful, your honour—wants pressing. He! he! he!

**Sir V.** Come, come, we must have no division in the house. You mustn't contradict your wife, friend Gilbert. Give her a kiss, and make it up at once!

**Alec.** Wi' all my heart!

(*Wiping his lips officiously preparatory, to Gilbert's great indignation.*)

**Pam.** (*Alarmed.*) No, no, no, no; there's no necessity for that.

**Gil.** (*Vehemently.*) Certainly not; no necessity at all—consarn it!

**Pam.** (*Aside.*) I see I must sing to restore harmony. (*Aloud.*) Well, if I must; but, indeed, I'm no singer.

**Sir V.** You'll do admirably well; we can't take any excuse.

**Pam.** You mustn't mind Cousin Alec, your honour. (*Looking affectionately at Gilbert.*) A little puts him out of the way. He's displeased with me, perhaps—thinks I ought to attend more to my husband. He should know me better. If I say little, I think the more; I have not forgotten the gipsy's warning when I went out a nutting.   A fair outside don't allure me; I look to the heart.   If that is sound, no matter how rough and homely the coat that covers it, 'tis all the same to me.

*Sir V.* You are a perfect angel, my dear, charming little Mistress Pamela! your voice shall carry it.   What say you, friends?

*Omnes.* Aye, aye;   Pamela's song.—Pamela's song!

*Sir V.* The Ayes have it!   Now then—hear, hear—we'll all join chorus!

BALLAD AND CHORUS.—PAMELA AND OMNES.

AIR.—" When we went out a gipsying."

PAMELA.

*As I was going a nutting, on a bright September day,*
*There came a sunburnt gipsy by, and thus I heard her say:*
*The birds sing merry on the bough, and thick the clusters grow,*
*Then listen to the gipsy's voice, as you a nutting go!*

CHORUS—OMNES.

*The birds sing merry on the bough, and thick the clusters grow,*
*Then listen to the gipsy's voice, as we a nutting go!*

PAMELA.

*The sun is shining warm and bright, and ready to the hand,*
*All fair and pleasant to the sight, the tempting wood nuts stand;*
*But, ah! my warning heed fair maids, while you your sports pursue,*
*For lovers are but mortal nuts, as coming years will show;*

CHORUS.—OMNES.

*The birds sing merry on the bough, and thick the clusters grow,*
*Then listen to the gipsy's voice, as you a nutting go!*

PAMELA.

*Ah! let not those too soon allure, who have a smooth outside,*
*For hollow and unsound, too oft, they prove with all their pride:*
*Reject not those that homely seem, however rough to view,*
*For ever they're most sound at heart, fair maids you'll find 'tis true.*

CHORUS.—OMNES.

*The birds sing merry on the bough, and thick the clusters grow,*
*Then listen to the gipsy's voice, as you a nutting go!*

(*Pamela sings this ballad in a marked manner, applying it designedly to Gilbert—it is warmly knocked down by the whole party.*)

*Sir V.* Bravo! very well sung indeed.   There's a nut to crack, for all of us.   Now all is peace and harmony again, I shall, therefore, as it is getting late, and you must be tired, leave you to your-

selves, and say, good-night—we shall meet in the morning.

[*Gilbert and Alec bow awkwardly—Dame and Pamela curtsey Sir Vivian off—who exits condescendingly. Servants, who have entered on Sir Vivian's departure, clear away any retire.*

*Gil.* (*Aside.*) In spite of all this, they bean't going to manage it in that manner, though.   It be all very well Baronet retiring, but I bean't going to retire—na, na—nor shall that fellow Alec, nor my Pamela retire neither—No, come what may, I'll be danged if my wife shall——

*Pam.* (*Aside to Gilbert, having overheard him.*) Be quiet, can't yon—when everybody is gone to rest, you shall find me waiting for you in the sleeping gallery—so come there and——

FRISBY *enters unperceived, and secretly listening, overhears what Pamela says.*

*Gil.* (*Aside to Pamela.*) Oh, oh! that be another thing—well, mind you do, if you don't I'll turn the whole Manor House topsy turvy, and I can tell you that.

*Pam.* I promise you.

*Fris.* (*Aside.*) What do I hear? an assignation between our little Pamela and her cousin? what's in the wind now?

*Dame.* Now, Pamela—(*Pamela crosses to Dame.*) —you know where you are to sleep, Alec.
                                                    (*To Gilbert.*)

*Gil.* Yes, yes—But I say, Dame——
                    (*Crosses after Pamela, seeing Alec making that way.*)

*Dame.* (*Aside to Gilbert.*) Fear nothing, I'll take care of Pamela, for you—(*Aloud.*)—Good night, good night——

                    (*Going, John and Thomas having mean-while got lights and lantern, they give lantern to Frisby, and prepare to light off Dame, Pamela, and Alec.*)

*Alec.* (*To Gilbert, marking after Pamela.*) Good night, cousin—He! ho!   I wish you a pleasant night's rest.   (*Sneeringly.*) Come, Pamela.

*Fris* (*To Gilbert.*) You know the way.
                    (*Gives lantern, and points off.*)

*Gil.* (*Discontentedly.*) Aye, nye, why didn't he give I a pitchfork as well as a lantern? there be those plaguy dogs.   (*Aside.*)   Good night—good night—good night, Pamela.   (*Aloud.*)

*Alec.* He, he, he!

                    [*Exit Dame, Alec, and Pamela, bowing and curtseying to Frisby, conducted by John and Thomas, on one side, Gilbert, with lantern, very unwill-ingly, on the other, leaving Frisby solus.*]

*Fris* (*After a short time.*) Oh! here the Baronet comes, it will save me seeking him.

*Re-enter* SIR VIVIAN, *in rich dressing-gown.*

Well, Sir Vivian, what do you think of our shep-herds and shepherdesses, sir?

*Sir V.* They have amused me immeasurably, Frisby.   Yaw—aw——                 (*Yawning.*)

*Fris.* Humph! and Pamela—what do you think of little Pamela?   Eh, sir?   (*With intention.*)

*Sir V.* She's enchanting—positively enchanting, Frisby.   What charms me most in her is, her de-lightful air of sincerity and innocence.—(*Frisby laughs.*)   Eh, what are you laughing at, Frisby?

*Fris.* (*Laughing ti'l he almost chokes himself.*) I beg your pardon, Sir Vivian, but I think you said *innocence!* and I could not help indulging in a smile, when I recollected the *tender assignation* I just now overheard pretty Mrs. Innocence make with her Cousin Alec, to steal out from the summer house and meet her in the bedroom gallery, when the poor fellow, her husband, is fast asleep, and not dreaming a word about the matter. If that's innocence, all I can say is, we've plenty of it in town.

*Sir V.* An assignation! you must be mad, Frisby—a veritable monomaniac.

*Fris.* Not at all, Sir Vivian—certain signals that I detected passing between Mrs. Pamela and our honest Cousin Alec, excited my suspicions—I approached them unobserved, and heard her promise to meet him in the sleeping gallery after everybody had retired to rest.

*Sir V.* You petrify me!—Pamela, whom I thought so pure!

*Fris.* You should never trust to appearances, Sir Vivian—those innocent faces are always the very devil when there's any love going on.

*Sir V.* Well, how one may be deceived! What's the use of being a legislator, and guarding morality.—Poor Gilbert! now I remember, I remarked something very odd about our cousin's manner, the time we were at supper.

*Fris.* Ha, ha, ha!—the poor devil of a husband —you ought, in my opinion, to endeavour to avenge him, Sir Vivian.

*Sir V.* I ought, I ought, Frisby—you are right, I'm bound to do it—morality, example—but how?

*Fris.* Oh, easily enough, sir. Substitute yourself for the expected gallant—you have only to steal to the sleeping gallery—this innocent little Pamela, no doubt, will take you for her cousin—thus you will soon be able to judge how far this unfortunate devil of a husband has been deceived, and expose the jade as she deserves.

*Sir V.* Admirable!—I'll do it!—Morality demands it.

*Fris.* You cannot do better, sir.

*Sir V.* But you must contrive somehow, Frisby, my good fellow, to prevent our cousin Alec, in the summer house, stealing out and spoiling all.

*Fris.* Oh, leave that to me, sir. I'll let the gardener's two great dogs loose, they'll stop him, I warrant me.

*Sir V.* Capital! excellent!—the very thing. I'll be off at once—mustn't forget the interests of morality—my duty, as a magistrate, as a legislator. —No, no!—Besides, a constituent's wife—duty, morality demands it.

*Fris.* Ha, ha! Bravo, Sir Vivian—and I'll go and unchain my friends, Cæsar and Dragon. So much for Mistress Innocence.

[*Exeunt Sir Vivian on one side, and Frisby, with lights, at the back.*

SCENE LAST—*Antique Sleeping Gallery in the Manor House, richly carved oak wainscoting of the Tudor period, running along the back of the stage, including a range of doors, leading to the different bedrooms.—It is dark.*

Enter JOHN and THOMAS, *with lights, conducting in* DAME, PAMELA, *and* ALEC.

*Tho.* (*Gives light to Dame.*) That is your room, madam. (*Points to door at right, and exits.*)
*John.* (*Giving light to Alec and Pamela, points to*

the other door on left.) That's the room for you and your good lady, sir.

*Alec.* (*Sniggering.*) Then me and my good lady will take possession on 'em—Ho, he, he!
(*Takes light, John bows and exits.*)

*Dame.* Well, now then, as all's arranged, we may as well retire at once. (*Pamela slips into the room that has been pointed out to Dame. Alec is furtively following her, when he is pulled back by Dame, who suddenly turns round and sees him.*) Hallo! what are you doing there, sir? You've no business there—that's no place for you, sir! that's your room. (*Pointing to the other room.*)

*Alec.* Ho, he, he! Dame, I wur only going to see if Pamela wur comfortable.

*Dame.* Safe bind, safe find.
(*Pushes Alec into the other room, closes door, and locks him in; she then follows Pamela into her own room, taking key of that with her. John and Thomas having disappeared, the stage is now left quite dark. Dame is heard carefully locking the door inside.*)

*After a short pause, enter* SIR VIVIAN, *in his dressing-gown, cautiously.*

*Sir V.* (*Soliloquising.*) As a representative of the people, it is incumbent on me to take Alec's place —yes, morality. (*At this moment door of Dame's room is heard cautiously unlocking.—Sir Vivian, in a low and cautious tone.*) Eh! don't I hear a door unlocking? Let me stand close a bit, to make sure; I must not discover myself till I am quite certain. (*Retires on one side.*)

*Enter* PAMELA, *cautiously, from Dame's room, having unlocked the door from within.*

*Pam.* (*Alarmed.*) I think all is clear—I hear no one—I am all in a twitter—my heart beats nineteen to the dozen. Alone, at this time of night, in the Manor House—I know not what to do. (*Sir Vivian making a movement to come forward, Pamela overhears him.*) Ha! who is this? Is that you, sweetheart?

*Sir V.* (*In a feigned voice.*) Yes, it's me.

*Pam.* (*Fondly mistaking him for Gilbert.*) How could you think I could possibly be unfaithful to you, dearest? How cruel it is of you to doubt me! You must not be jealous of your cousin; I hate him. Your Pamela is yours alone!

*Sir V.* I believe you. (*Aside.*) The deceitful jade!—that poor devil of a husband! Here's morality!

*Enter* GILBERT, *groping his way at back, minus one of the skirts of the tail of his coat.*

*Gil.* (*In a cautious voice.*) Those cantankerous dogs! Dang that Cæsar!—he seized I fast enough, How could they get loose, I wonder? Left tail of my coat behind me—I could hardly get away from him—I wur obliged to leave tail of my coat, and glad to get off so well—lucky it warn't anything else. Well, I mun manage to feel my way somehow. (*Gropes about.*)

*Sir V.* (*Not seeing Gilbert.*) Dear Pamela, grant me but one little kiss!

*Pam.* (*Still mistaking Sir Vivian for Gilbert.*) Take two, with pleasure—I can refuse you nothing.

*Gil.* (*Astounded, advancing close to Pamela, at the moment Sir Vivian kisses her.*) Twenty thousand devils! So I ha' come to hear this, be I?

*Pam.* (*Quickly, feeling the height of Sir Vivian.*) Heavens! this is not Gilbert!

*Gil.* (*Furiously.*) Yes, it be Gilbert, cockatrice! But the Baronet shall be made acquainted wi' all your criminy con. false heartedness; ho shall know of your fine goings on. I'll raise the whole Manor House — have all the fortin to mysen. Here! murder — robbery — fire — thieves — mad dogs!

*Sir V.* (*Aside.*) Confound him! he'll wake everybody!

*Pam.* (*Frightened.*) Mercy on me! what have I done?

*Gil.* (*Calling loudly.*) Dame—Sir Vivian—Mr. Frisby—lights—house—Cæsar—Dragon!

*Enter* DAME, *from room, in night-dress, with candle*—FRISBY, THOMAS, *and* JOHN, *half-dressed, followed by other Servants, also with chamber candles, from different sides. Stage light.*

*Dame.* What in the name of Heaven is the matter? What's all this bawling for? Pamela, child, why are you out of bed? I was in the sweetest sleep——

*Gil.* (*Who has not seen Sir Vivian.*) I didn't bawl without reason, Dame. I ha' just caught my wife here wi' some infernal scoundrel — some damned rascal——

*Sir V.* (*who has been slinking in the background*) *and Fris.* His wife!

*Dame.* (*Aside, to Gilbert.*) There! you've done it—there goes the hundred pounds!

*Sir V.* (*To Gilbert, coming forward.*) What! Cousin Alec, is Pamela your wife?

*Gil.* (*Desperately.*) Not Cousin Alec, but Cousin Gilbert himself, sir. If the truth mun be told, Pamela be my wife; and now, then, there be an end on't.

*Sir V.* Why, then, the other Gilbert——

*Gil.* Be only the cousin that I wur to be, Mr. Baronet, sir.

*Alec.* (*Within.*) Let me out—let me out!

(*Beating violently against his bed-room door. Frisby opens door, and lets Alec out. He has hastily dressed himself, and has his nightcap on.*)

*Sir V.* I see it all! Dame, you have deceived me!

*Pam.* Oh, your honour, pray forgive my mother! The fact is, Gilbert was absent when you sent for my husband, and said he must come with me to receive my fortune; and fearful of losing it, we introduced Cousin Alec in his stead, and I agreed to meet Gilbert here, when all were asleep, to prevent his having any more jealousy about the matter.

*Sir V.* Ha, ha, ha! A capital joke, faith, and I—you must forgive me laughing at you, Gilbert—I can assure you I only took your place from a sense of duty—the interests of morality. As a moral man and legislator, you know I——

*Gil.* (*Drily.*) Oh yes, yes, I knows; it be all right, your honour—(*Aside*)—that is, as it happened to turn out. Though what morality ha' to do wi' kissing I don't know.

*Sir V.* (*To Dame.*) I ought to punish your want of confidence in me, Dame; but this little plot of yours has been the means of amusing me too much to allow me to be seriously angry; and as there has been no entrenchment on morality—for I'm very particular on that score—I forgive all; and to prove it, there is the hundred pounds I promised you. Take it, and may you be happy with it!

(*Takes out purse and gives money to Gilbert.*)

*Pam. and Dame.* (*Curtseying.*) Oh, your honour!

*Gil.* (*Taking Pamela's hand.*) Long life to your honour! (*Puts money into his breeches pocket—aside.*) I'm glad I've got my wife and the hundred pounds too.

*Sir V.* We can now retire once more to rest. Having resigned honest Gilbert his wife, you, Alec, must be content to take his place in the summer-house.

*Gil.* (*Exultingly.*) Aye, aye, along wi' Cæsar and Dragon. Mind your coat-tail. Ha, ha, ha!

(*Laughs.*)

*Alec.* (*Coolly.*) Oh, I don't care! It bean't my coat; it be yours, you know. He, he, he!

(*Ruefully forces a laugh.*)

*Sir V.* The mastiffs shall be fastened up. No doubt, we shall all sleep comfortably enough after these little adventures.

*Pam.* Oh yes, your honour, very comfortably! If all our friends are only as good as your honour, and, taking the will for the deed, will kindly excuse poor Pamela any little error she may have committed in——

*Gil.* (*Significantly.*) In Borrowing a Husband! and Sleeping Out!

(*Parties form Tableau.*)

CURTAIN.

,